TOP TRADE CAREERS

IT TECHNICIAN

A Crabtree Branches Book

B. Keith Davidson

CRABTREE
Publishing Company
www.crabtreebooks.com

School-to-Home Support for Caregivers and Teachers

This high-interest book is designed to motivate striving students with engaging topics while building fluency, vocabulary, and an interest in reading. Here are a few questions and activities to help the reader build upon his or her comprehension skills.

Before Reading:

- *What do I think this book is about?*
- *What do I know about this topic?*
- *What do I want to learn about this topic?*
- *Why am I reading this book?*

During Reading:

- *I wonder why...*
- *I'm curious to know...*
- *How is this like something I already know?*
- *What have I learned so far?*

After Reading:

- *What was the author trying to teach me?*
- *What are some details?*
- *How did the photographs and captions help me understand more?*
- *Read the book again and look for the vocabulary words.*
- *What questions do I still have?*

Extension Activities:

- *What was your favorite part of the book? Write a paragraph on it.*
- *Draw a picture of your favorite thing you learned from the book.*

TABLE OF CONTENTS

IN MY COMMUNITY

A community is a group of people living and working together. It is groups of people coming together with the common purpose of making their city or town a better place to live.

Each person
has a role to
play, and all
community
members rely
on each other.

An Information Technology technician, also known as an IT technician, plays an important role in that community. The IT technician repairs our technology and installs the devices and **software** that we use every day to connect with the world.

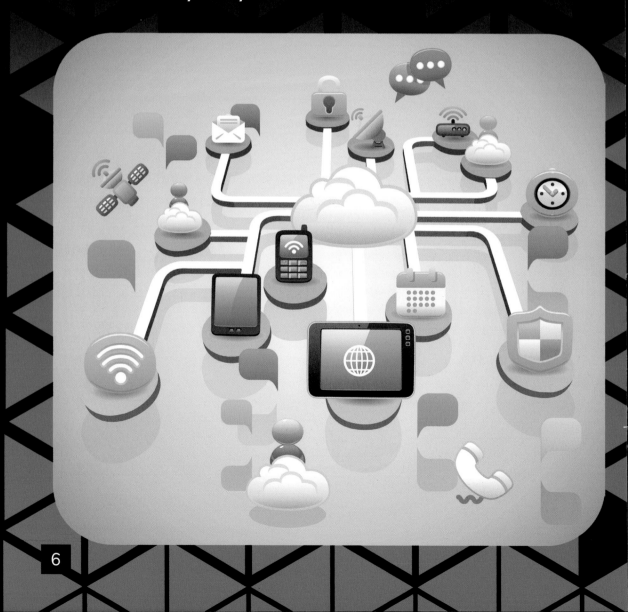

WHAT DO I NEED TO BE AN IT TECHNICIAN?

A knowledge of computers and technology is a good start to becoming an IT technician. For some IT positions, a high school diploma and a certificate from a community college is all you need.

Other companies prefer to hire applicants with a four-year degree in a computer-related field. Many companies are willing to train IT technicians on the job.

SPECIAL SKILLS

IT technicians help people with their computer issues. They need excellent communication skills to give clear instructions. In many cases, the technician is working **remotely** and relying on information from users who have little technical knowledge.

IT technicians must also be **certified** in special programs related to software, operating systems, or even the industry that their company is servicing.

What's the difference between an IT technician and a computer programmer? Computer programmers design software and write code. IT technicians install software and maintain computers and networks.

Sometimes the problem is with the computer's **hardware**, or its parts, and sometimes it is with the software. The technician must understand how software works with different computers. Sometimes viruses can spread between computers. Viruses are designed to harm the computer or steal information.

When a computer has been hacked, it means someone other than the user has gained control over it. Hackers do this by installing **malware** without the computer's user knowing about it.

System HACKED

IT technicians need a basic understanding of many different industries. Health, sales, and entertainment are just a few industries that have specific software and hardware needs.

Business-specific software companies usually have their own training programs for IT technicians. Because of the industry standards, technicians need to know how to do this work.

The technician needs to understand how these technologies work, and how to **optimize** them for their **clients**.

WORKING CONDITIONS

Some IT technicians work in offices. Many IT technicians work remotely, in call centers, or in their own homes. They receive calls from clients about problems.

They either access the client's computer remotely or talk the client through the problem. This can mean long hours on the phone.

Other IT technicians travel to businesses or to people's houses to fix computer problems.

They may visit several homes or businesses in a day.

Computer stores also employ IT technicians at their locations to help customers. These IT technicians can help customers choose computers, printers, and other devices. They can help explain software and how to install it.

The U.S. Bureau of Labor Statistics predicts a 13 percent growth in computer-related jobs in the next 10 years. That's higher than overall job growth.

Wherever a technician works, the job remains the same. IT technicians help people and businesses connect their devices and software and make sure that everything runs smoothly.

Some IT technicians are green experts too. New technology is making our world a greener place and IT technicians are helping connect companies with software and devices that make them more efficient.

THE CHALLENGES YOU WILL FACE

There are always challenges with any job, and an IT technician's job is no different. For example, some software only works on certain devices.

Some clients want their technology to work in a way it was not designed to work.

A REWARDING CAREER

Working as an IT technician is a rewarding career. You connect people to the world through their technology and make a good living at the same time. However, the salary normally depends on the industry.

Specialty	Salary Range Per Year
Telecommunications	$68,000 - $74,220
Non-Residential	$63,000 - $68,500
Specialty Trade	$56,000 - $61,700
Residential	$46,950 - $50,000

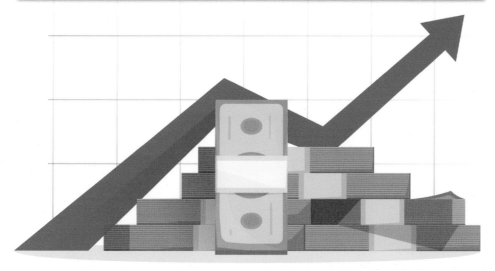

Working as an IT technician is a growing field that offers many exciting opportunities for people of all backgrounds and skill levels. It is also an important job as every home and business uses technology. It makes this career path a solid choice for anyone who loves computers and technology.

certified (SUR-tuh-fyed): someone with certificates proving their skills and training

clients (KLY-uhnts): people who pay for the services of others

code (KOHD): the special language written for and used in computers

hardware (HARD-wair): computers, laptops, smartphones, and tablets; the devices we use to access software programs

malware (MAL-wair): programs designed to damage computers

networks (NET-wurks): sets of two or more computers that are connected with one another for the purpose of sharing information

optimize (OP-ti-MYZE): to make something work efficiently

remotely: (ri-MOHT-lee): from another location

software (SAWFT-wair): programs designed for computers

WEBSITES TO VISIT

www.bls.gov/ooh/computer-and-information-technology/computer-support-specialists.htm#tab-1

https://blog.transparentcareer.com/college-students/career-guides/5-facts-working-tech

www.wgu.edu/blog/it-glossary-tech-tools-kids2001.html

ABOUT THE AUTHOR

B. Keith Davidson

B. Keith Davidson has had careers in agriculture, industrial manufacturing, and the service industry. His career in education led to his current career in writing books.

Written by: B. Keith Davidson

Designed by: Jennifer Dydyk

Edited by: Kelli Hicks

Proofreader: Ellen Rodger

Print and production coordinator:
Katherine Berti

Library and Archives Canada Cataloguing in Publication

Available at the Library and Archives Canada

Library of Congress Cataloging-in-Publication Data

Available at the Library of Congress

Crabtree Publishing Company

www.crabtreebooks.com   1-800-387-7650

Published in the United States
Crabtree Publishing
347 Fifth Avenue
Suite 1402-145
New York, NY, 10016

Published in Canada
Crabtree Publishing
616 Welland Ave.
St. Catharines, ON
L2M 5V6

Printed in the U.S.A./CG20210915/012022